Guide to the Craft
Of
Surveillance

A Beginner's Book for the Professional

Robert Estes, CPI

Dedicated to my wife, Debra Estes,
whose joy and enthusiasm embraces me and our lives.

CONTENTS

Beginner's Guide to the Art of Surveillance

This is a handbook for those interested in the Private Investigator profession and the delicate and determined art of Sub-rosa Surveillance. It is also useful for the PIs who need a refresher course.

It details what one needs to know about what one needs to know.

Herein are succinct, concise chapters and a How-To list for newbies and Old-bies attracted by the fascinating career of a Private Investigator.

Read, reflect, and reach...

YOU can be a PI!

CHAPTER ONE

You are thinking of Becoming a Private Investigator Because...

You have a <u>Curious</u> mind. You are <u>Observant</u>. You look about and see things that others miss. You don't blink; you think. You have an ability to see beyond what it is front of you, but don't overlook the forest for the trees. You are <u>Creative</u>. You can <u>Improvise.</u> You have <u>Dexterity.</u> You have <u>Tenacity.</u> You are <u>Fearless</u>, but not foolish. And, above all, you are <u>Truthful.</u>

Those are the qualities you need to possess to become a successful <u>Private Investigator.</u>

There are many different paths to the profession. Some start in Law Enforcement, others in the Military. Some come to it through classes specifically tailored to the field. Many have started with existing investigative firms. It takes a plan and persistence to enjoy a career in this rewarding vocation.

There are many different disciplines of detective work. Worker's Compensation Fraud, Domestic, Child and Elder Abuse, Civil and Criminal litigation, Background checks, Statement taking, Witness location, Loss prevention, Bug sweeping, etc.

This guidebook concentrates on The Art of Surveillance and Sub-rosa, an intriguing part of the science of Investigation.

We will take you through chapters on what equipment you will need, how to set up surveillance, how to follow your subject, what to do if you lose him or her, and other essentials of Investigation.

So, set your sights to Sub-rosa!

CHAPTER TWO

Before you consider the career

There are certain capabilities and equipment that are essential to successful surveillance:

- Own a reliable vehicle that is appropriate for surveillance (a Van or SUV is best, but sometimes a non-descript sedan works well, too. Best to have both available)
- Be insured
- Own a computer/laptop
- Own a cell phone
- Own a printer/scanner
- Have internet access at home, office, and in the field
- Be proficient in computer word processing operating systems such MS Word, Mac, Excel, and others
- Be able to write in a concise yet descriptive manner
- Know Be familiar with on-line search engines such as Internet Explorer, Mozilla, Firefox, Google Chrome
- Know at least a little about video cameras and photography
- Know how to upload reports and videos to Dropbox, Hightail, and other sharing sites.
- Know how to convert video so that it has a Time/Date stamp

- Be able to follow instructions
- Be able to be improvise and be calm in difficult situations
- Have a credit card/ATM card that will allow you access to cash
- Be able to go out of town

And do not have a criminal record.

CHAPTER THREE

Checklist for Success

The ability to conduct Sub-rosa and Surveillance investigations is a fundamental and rewarding part of being a licensed Private Investigator. Those who excel at it are always in demand and they find satisfaction in a job well done. Offered here is checklist of what to do before you start the case.

First and Foremost-   Know Your Assignment!

The Five Ws + an H: Who What Where When Why How

- What: Kind of Investigation
  1. Worker's Compensation
  2. Domestic

- Who: Know your subject! Check Social Media, Google, etc.
    1. Facebook My Space Instagram, Tindr, etc.

- Where: Know the residence and surroundings
    1. Google Maps, Earth, etc.
    2. Are there malls/parks/medical buildings nearby?

- Why: Know why you are working this case and the expectations
    1. Observation and documentation of activities
    2. Video evidence

- When: All times concerned with the case
    1. Period of prior circumstances
    2. Start time for Surveillance

- How: How to you plan to conduct the investigation
    1. Surveillance
    2. Internet
    3. Court Searches, etc.

Vehicles

- Have a neutral color SUV or van with dark windows or curtains.
- No ads on license plate frame or any bumper stickers
- Make sure vehicle is in excellent condition! Can't break down in the middle of surveillance!
- Window cleaner and paper towels

- Make sure the tank is FULL before and when you get there
- Have a second vehicle available. A non-descript sedan is always useful.
- Be prepared to rent a vehicle if out of town.

Cameras

- HD models with HDSD cards
- Back up camcorder
- Back up batteries/car charger capable
- HDSD cards
- Still Camera 14 Meg pixels (just in case)

Covert Cameras

- Self-Contained DVR pin hole with time/date stamp
- Mini SD card ones such as keychain or sunglasses
- Thumb drive, pen or wristwatch

Video Transfer

- Dropbox Dazzle, YouSendit or other choice
- Wi-Fi, upload from camera

Cell Phone/Tablet

- All field Wi-Fi access capability for internet research
- Data Providers i.e., TLO, IRB, Tracers, DMV, etc.
- Pre-Paid Calling Card or Trac-fone for pretexts

Notebook

- Pen/pencil
- Notebook

Equipment

- Tripod/Monopod
- GPS
- Binoculars/Monocular   Night Vision

Props

- Flyers for lost animals
- Religious pamphlets
- Receipt book
- Camouflage Clothing/hats
- Yellow vest/clipboard
- Camp chair
- Add your own!

Clothing
- Packed suitcase for a couple of days
- Gym bag with appropriate workout clothes
- Shorts, t shirt
- Slacks, Dress Shirt
- Dress

- Appropriate shoes

Food

- Water
- Snacks

Personal

- Medications
- Sunscreen
- Toiletries
- Porta-Potty or other way for evacuation of waste
- Heat can be a problem: Remember it's usually 10 degrees or more hotter inside your vehicle than outside: keep an ice chest or other items that may help cool you down.

Safety

- Pepper Spray
- Tire Iron (just kidding)

Cash

- $100.00 at least!
- Credit card

Travel

- AAA card or similar
- FasTrak
- Clipper Card (or local similar public transport card)
- **Passport (hey, ya never know!)**

Sub-rosa and Surveillance is a demanding and tricky endeavor. The best Professionals are prepared for anything....
And then some.

CHAPTER FOUR

The First Day

The first day of a new case is always exciting.

You've got your assignment. You've been provided with a name, an address, and a goal. Before setting out, you should always double check the Sub-rosa Survival list...

Then-

Get there **EARLY**! Many people must drive far distances to get to work. If you want to start surveillance at 6:00 AM, get there at 5:30 AM.

Now-

The **RESIDENCE**. Where is it located? In an older neighborhood? Lower income? Middle income? Sub-division? Gated apartment complex? High income? Rural or remote? Even if you have been there before, things may have changed. Take nothing for granted.

Which lights are lit, if any. Are drapes closed/open? Any newspapers in the driveway or at the curb? Is it a two-car garage with one car off to the side? Do the vehicles look operable? Are there any on-going projects? Is the landscaping well-tended? Are there children's toys in the yard? Beware of Dog sign? Fenced back yard? Boat? Signs on the yard advocating political candidates? Are there balloons on the mail post? Maybe a Birthday party today. Check the telephone posts and light standards on the way there; garage/yard sale today/coming up? In the neighborhood?

The **NEIGHBORS**: Do the neighbors have on-going projects that might keep them outside for extended periods, allowing them to take extra notice of your vehicle? Are their garages open? Do they have chairs inside garage where they sit and watch the day go by? Are there gang symbols on the fences? If in a rural area, is there agriculture business and lots of traffic?

The **VEHICLES**. Do not drive up and down the street trying to get license plates. That will get you noticed like a pimple on a prom queen. If there are several vehicles, walk by (once) dressed in dark clothing and be nondescript. Note if the vehicles have bumper stickers, i.e., "My Child is Student of week at...." or political statements or sports teams.

The **SET UP LOCATION**.   Your best scenario is a secluded spot where you can observe the front door, yard and exits. This ideal opportunity doesn't happen often, however. Second best is a locale where you can see the vehicles depart the driveway or curb. If that is not possible, then sit where the most likely exit may be observed. Remember it is always easier to move up and get video than to get noticed before you start. You don't want to have to drive by every hour to check for activity, but if necessary, do so discreetly and do not make U-turns.

The **TEMPERATURE.** It's gonna get hot. No matter what season or what the temperature is outside, it's gonna be hot sitting in the back of a van or SUV. Look for shade; it helps you stay unobserved and helps you keep cool. Be prepared with water and a cooling system like a neck wrap which has been soaked water and frozen. Don't play the radio. Don't watch videos. Don't smoke. Don't make phone calls. Text, if needed, to correspond to your client.

The **CALL**. Notify local law enforcement and let them know who you are and where you will be conducting stationary surveillance. A caveat: probably best not to call if the person in question is in law enforcement or you know that the city in question checks out every call anyway.

The **FIVE SENSES**. Sight! What do you see in front of you, what is nearby? Hearing! Listen and pay attention! The buzz of machinery may indicate lawn mowing or a leaf blower. Did a car start? Shouting may mean a disturbance at the residence or nearby. Your ears are as essential as your eyes. Scent! What do you smell? BBQ? Tar -roofing? Long-standing filth? Taste! may come into play if the subject works at a restaurant and serves diners. Touch! May be important to determine heat on a vehicle that has been recently used. Be aware that all **5 Senses** should be used accordingly to appropriateness.

The **DIFFICULT SITS**. The troublesome sits include apartment complexes that have the doors to the units facing in and to a common area not visible from the street or inside. Mobile Home parks may have the same situations. It's always nice to have a vehicle for your subject, but sometimes you don't. Try to locate a visitor space or an empty carport space that affords a look at the front door or exit ways. You can always move if someone comes. Some upscale complexes may have roaming security guards. Think and act like you belong there. Do not fear. You can leave if it gets heated up. If you see the subject approach his vehicle, that's the time to leave so you don't immediately follow them out of the complex. Difficult sits may even be in areas where it seems so cozy, but, alas, there is no street parking allowed. But, there might be a house for sale on the block and you can park in the driveway.

Look, assess, and determine what will work.

> **GATED** communities include sub-divisions, apartment complexes, and mobile home parks.

Looks impossible, but it can be done. Most security gates rise and fall within a few seconds; time enough to scurry yourself in and check the surroundings. Some gates do not allow a second vehicle easily and you might have to walk in while someone else is walking out. Be sure to collect all information needed while inside, i.e., vehicles, description of residence, any projects, etc. You may not be able to remain inside the area and worse: There may be several ways out. In that instance, make sure you have checked the most appropriate exit. Understand that sometimes it takes more than one investigator to successfully negotiate getting a subject out of a gated area.

RURAL and REMOTE SITES. California is a big state with lots of different terrain and territories. Canyons, beaches, rivers, redwoods, desert, and all possible conditions that make surveillance darn near impossible can apply. Once again, you must know where you are. Check Google Earth or aerial photos. Ask local businesses or homeowners how to get in and out of where you are. It's likely you will have to establish surveillance a distance away from the subject's home. Know the main arteries to get to freeways, malls, sub-divisions, medical buildings. Check for sites above the target's home. Check to see if you can watch while on foot and get back to your vehicle in time, if the subject leaves.

Difficult sits may even be in areas where it seems so cozy, but, alas, there is no street parking allowed. But, there might be a house for sale on the block and you can park in the driveway. Look, assess, and determine what will work.

Always keep in mind, the assignment and what you will need to do to follow through to offer the best results to the client. The **FIRST DAY** will set the tone for the investigation. This is not a career for the timid or the foolhardy or the mindless machismo. We are professionals, performing with determination and dignity.

CHAPTER FIVE

"On The Move!"

<u>Anticipate</u> but don't <u>Assume</u>!

FIRST and FORMOST: Always start the day with a full tank of gas. You don't know where you'll end up....

Here are some different scenarios you may face:

Your target has left on foot. Now what?
How is he/she dressed? Are they in a jogging suit? Business clothes? Carrying a briefcase, laptop, suitcase? With others, or children, or dogs?
This will determine your next decision. You should know beforehand where the local bus stops or municipal transportation stations are located. Are they within walking distance?

Should you depart from your vehicle? No public transportation nearby? Then maybe subject is just out for a walk or jog. In that case, stay in your vehicle and back away so as not to alert the subject. Note that most people don't look back. They look side to side.

If Public transportation is within walking distance and if the subject looks like he is going somewhere, then be prepared. Make sure you have change, cash, or best, a public transportation card like Clipper. Have your cell phone GPS with you so you know where you are and can get back to your vehicle.

If the Subject leaves on bicycle or motorcycle, be aware that bikes can go where cars cannot. Have a stationary camera on your dashboard, if possible, to record the movements. Keep in mind that someone on a bicycle may take mapped routes and might end up in the same usual places that a car can go...only takes a bit longer. Motorcycles are a special challenge and it is best to know the subject and their habits.

If the Subject leaves in a vehicle: What kind? What type of person? Is it an SUV/4WD that may indicate traveling distances or in a rural area? Truck/pickup? Anything in the bed? Note that most SUV and pickups have smaller back windows and it's harder to see someone following them. Side windows are used for larger trucks; therefore, you may stay directly behind them. Prius/Hybrid/HOV vehicles may be going to work and can go into the HOV lanes. Best technique is to keep to the right of the vehicle, if possible. Most drivers look to the rear-view mirror and the left side mirror. When possible, keep a vehicle between you and the subject. This is not always available, especially in city conditions.

City Conditions: Large cities and even mid-sized cities have lights on every block in downtown and other shopping areas. In these situations, the driver is usually focused directly ahead or to the side. You should try to stay as close as possible. Note if the driver checks the rear-view mirror obsessively. Keep your sunshade visor down. Do not let the driver/subject make eye contact. A quick turn of the signal can happen and you've lost them. There may be times when it seems that you are tethered to the back fender of the subject's car; stay with it until you can put a vehicle between you two. If you hit a red light and the subject goes through, try to turn right and make a U-turn sideways to get around the cars waiting to go the other way. But NEVER put yourself or other drivers in harm's way.

Freeway tailing: It is as easy to lose visual contact on the freeway as it is on city streets. Some subjects race as if they were at Indy. Others slow down as if they were looking for a lost kitten. Some will weave in and out of traffic just to get a car ahead. When backed up at commute time, keep close; the subject will be looking forward trying to get an advantage. Sometimes you may have to nudge yourself over to one side or the other and inch in where others tread, and they may honk or be angry. Be not afraid, they will get over it. Keep your eyes on the prize.

Sub-division tailing: Winding lanes through neighborhoods are common. If you stay too close, the subject might catch on but too far back, you lose them. Note that most vehicles have some sort of identifying mark. Keep an eye out for courts and circles, if you don't see them right away, travel back and check the outskirts.

Rural tailing: Long/lonely lumpy/bumpy roads over dirt/gravel/unpaved lanes without a clue to where you may end up have complications too. The subject knows where he/she is going...you don't. Staying too close alerts them, staying too far back leaves you without a sniff of the trail. In daylight, you might be able to hang back and watch the dust; at night, you might see the headlights turn in the distance. Keep your GPS on and use it to assist you in identifying where you are and where they may go.

Got 'em where you want 'em

Commercial buildings: Industrial buildings may not have access to those who are not employed there. Keep an eye out for exits. The subject may change clothes or leave in a different vehicle with other people. Always note the physical characteristics of your target and take video or stills for identification.

Inside Malls: Subjects tend not to look up. If the mall has an upper floor, try following them from above. You can also keep track by looking at reflections in shop windows so you don't have to directly look at the target.

Grocery/retail Stores: Subjects tend to look side to side up and down rarely behind.

Parks/Playgrounds: Subjects may be with children. If so, and you are videotaping, try to use a covert camera or at least make sure that others don't notice you. People are very aware of situations where children may be involved and may alert your target.

Restaurants/Clubs/Bars: These are usually crowded. Sometimes that is good, as they may not pay attention to you, but also it may be a problem if you do not get good sight lines. Bars usually have mirrors on the back wall and you may use that to watch the target. Booths may be available in restaurants or tables by the doors. Try not to sit near restrooms as the target may use them and walk by you.

Paid venues: The subject may go to a sporting event, music event or other inside stadium or auditorium setting. If tickets are not available at the door, scalpers may be nearby. If you can't get it, determine the exits. Find out if the event is televised or being videotaped. It may be possible to get copies.

Active Participation: Circumstances may be that your target is playing a sport or in a recital or such. Usually this is not a problem, however, some venues do not allow videotaping and one must be discreet.

Hat Tricks and Disguises

Always keep handy a little something to change your looks. It may be a hat, different clothing, wigs, or sometimes just a change of hairstyle. Be creative and use whatever is applicable for the situation.

Following someone is the most challenging discipline of the investigator. It takes the nerves of a burglar and the concentration of surgeon. Usually, you don't get a second chance if you lose your target. It's thrilling and exciting, which is why most of us keep coming back to it. It's an art and a skill. Stay at it, keep practicing and you'll find it rewarding both spiritually and financially.

CHAPTER SIX

You lost 'em! Now what?

There is nothing more frustrating for an investigator than to lose a subject while following him or her. It happens to all of us; the key is to find them after you have lost 'em. Sub-rosa/Surveillance is an adventure, not for the faint-hearted or week-kneed. Perseverance and a keen eye are essential.

DETERMINATION. DON'T GIVE UP! Most people are creatures of habit and tend to go to the same places, follow the same routes, go to the same friend's homes, and have a pattern of consistency. Be PREPARED!

YOUR MODIS OPERANDI.   Have an appropriate vehicle, one that allows you to sit higher than the rest of traffic. Vans and SUVs are especially good for this.   Utilize a vehicle that can make sharp U-turns, a vehicle that can speed up quickly. Use a vehicle with a GPS system that has a grid map available and keep your position on at all times. Many vehicles have a GPS built into the dashboard, otherwise use a stand-alone model. Don't forget that most cell phones have this capability, too.

FOREWARNED IS FOREARMED.

Know thy subject!

- Age? What activities normal for the age group?

- Dating? Check Social Media.
- Do they work? Where?
- Are they Married? Does the spouse work? Where?
- Any children? What ages? Where are the nearest schools/playgrounds/sports venues?
- Relatives?
- Do parents live in the area?
- Hobbies? Do they hunt, fish, play sports, work-out or practice Yoga?
- Ethic Background? Some cities have distinct districts of cultural concerns.

Know the Vehicle

- Ensure that you have the license plate and identifiers as many vehicles look the same in the midst of traffic.
- Does the vehicle have any bumper stickers that provide a clue: "My child is an honor student at……", political stickers, AA, etc.
- Note any anomalies such as a gun rack or a personalized license plate frame. All may indicate a hobby, a church or other affiliation.

Know Where You Are

- Before you initiate surveillance, Google the residence and streets to get a view of where you are.

- Arrive early!
- Check the cross streets: Are there dead ends, work projects, is it a sub-division? Gated? How many exits?
- Note the location of nearby businesses: Grocery Stores Malls, Medical Offices, Hospitals, Playgrounds, Day-Care Centers, Dog parks, Schools, Flea Markets, Movie theaters, popular restaurants and Ethnic cultural spots.

KEEP YOUR COOL So the subject has driven away from the residence and you've lost sight of 'em. Now what?

- Where did they go?
- How was the subject dressed? Pajamas? Business suit? Casual? Formal? Work-out? That will give a clue to where the subject might go: Work, appointment, shopping, etc.
- Who's in the vehicle? Alone? Kids? Spouse? Friend? Parent? Dog? That provides a clue as to their destination: School, Daycare, Private Residence, Playground, Dog park, etc.

FIND THEM If you are driving along a busy street and lose sight because cars are between you and them, and you can't see ahead or when you do they are not there, look to the right. It is easier for them to make a right turn at a light than a left turn. Keep turning right on cross streets as it is more likely that they are able to keep going that way.

If the subject enters a subdivision with lots of winding and small streets, use your GPS to get a quick look at the exits, then make a grid search by going up and down each street. Most oftentimes, the subject will be parked on the street at the curb, but be sure to eye the driveways as well.

In a rural area, look for kicked up dust or freshly laid down grass. Many rural areas have long driveways that are private and you can't go down each and every one. In a gated area, has the gate just closed?

Lost in Freeway traffic due to gridlock? Keep going…. They are probably backed up too. Note the off ramps as they are usually congested and you might see them there just waiting for you! But Be Safe! Don't cause accidents by being over aggressive towards other drivers.

If subject has distinct ethnic characteristics, try checking cultural areas for shopping, dining, sports, worship, etc.

WATCH THE CLOCK Pay attention to the time of day.

6:00 AM to 9:00 AM. The subject may be going to work. Check nearby business parks, strip malls, or merchant areas. The subject may be going for coffee or breakfast. Where is the nearest Starbucks or donut shop? The subject may be going to the gym. Where is the closest? Are there children in the vehicle? Where is the closest school?

10:00 AM to 1:00 PM. The subject may be going to an appointment. Check nearby medical plazas, law offices, or other professional buildings. The subject may be grocery shopping so check the nearby stores' parking lots.

11:00 AM to 3:00 PM. The subject may be going to appointments. Check as previously described. The subject may be going to a restaurant. Check nearby shopping centers and eateries.

2:00 PM to 6:00 PM. The subject may be shopping or picking up kids. Check the previous noted locations.

6:00 PM to 9:00 PM. The subject may be out to dinner; check nearby restaurants. The subject may be attending a sports events or visiting friends. Do a grid search of the area.

8:00 PM to 12:00 AM. The subject may be out for the evening. Check bars and local nighttime recreational areas.

NEVER ON A SUNDAY   The day of the week matters, too!

- Saturday: Sports, shopping, family gatherings, garage sales.
- Sunday: Church services, parks and recreation, garage sales, family events.

- Special Events: Is there something going on locally? Farmer's Market? Parade? Flea Market? Make sure you know what is happening in your subject's home area. Check hometown newspapers and posted flyers.

It is a challenging profession we have chosen. Keep a keen eye and practice peripheral vision. Experience provides that the subject is more likely to be in the conspicuous spot than the hidden one.

"If you lose 'em, remember that if you see hoof prints, think horses before zebras."

But DAMN nice to catch the zebra on the loose, too.

CHAPTER SEVEN

The REPORT!

Your report is a sacred document. It is a **LEGAL** document. It may be used by opposing council. Your report should be exact, written with times and activities. It must be free of personal bias. Write in a third person narrative and do not use 'I". Your report should not make interpretive comments like the claimant grasped his leg in pain or the subject kissed the male with passion.

Your report should tell the truth, not tell a tale. This is the bond between you and your client. Let your words and the evidence show the way. The client will decide.

Your clients will probably have a report format that they prefer.

Be prepared that all will be included in some form:

- **Claimant/Subject name and address**
- **Departure time from office**
- **Start Date/Time**
- **Description of residence including any projects or unusual items**
- **Description and license plates of vehicles, including owner if known**
- **Location of surveillance set up.**
- **Hourly or as directed updates, including whether by walk-by or drive-by**
- **Claimant description when first noted, including any orthopedic devices, and clothing**
- **Clear description of activity and times**
- **Mail delivery or trash pick up**
- **Addresses and descriptions of locations visited.**
- **Vehicles and plates of those who visited claimant residence**
- **Vehicles and plates at residences that claimant visited**
- **Description of activity**

- Notation of obtained video/or why no video obtained
- If lost visual, explain where and why. Explain methods to locate
- End of report reads when and why surveillance was discontinued. i.e. no activity, lost, office direction
- Summary of video and depiction of activity
- Time/Miles/Expenses/Video

CHAPTER EIGHT

REPORT TEMPLATE

Ivona XXXXX
100 Main ST.
San Jose, CA 95136

Sunday, November 23, 2014

6:30 AM: We arrive in the vicinity of the claimant's residence at 100 Main St., San Jose. It is a single story single family dwelling, blue in color, with an attached two car garage. It is located in a middle-income neighborhood of similar homes. There is a front yard and lawn, neat and trim. There are children's bicycles by the front door. The back yard is fenced and cannot be seen from the street. Drapes to the windows of the house are closed and no activity is noted. Parked in the driveway is a gray KIA SUV, CA# 7BNYXXX, registered to Carmen Julia XXXX. Next to it is a blue Dodge Neon sedan, CA# 5PVSXXX, registered to Isiah XXXX. Surveillance is established on Maple Way where the driveway and front yard are visible.

8:00 AM: No change or activity is noted.

9:37 AM: A male Hispanic, 50's, exits the house and is by the KIA. A female Hispanic, 50's, also exits the house goes to the driver's door. Three children, ages 10 and 6 and 2 are now outside. The claimant exits the house and is by the right rear passenger door. She lets the children in and then gets in herself. The older female drives them from the area.

The claimant is described as a Hispanic female, 27 years old, 5'5", 120 lbs. with long black hair. She is wearing a black long sleeved top and black jeans. She is wearing heeled boots and does not have an orthopedic device on her right foot.
(Portions on video)

9:45 AM: They arrive at Calvary Church at 1175 Hillsdale Ave., San Jose. They park in the lot behind the church. A few minutes later, they all get out and walk towards the church complex. The claimant is with the 3 children and they walk to and enter the Bible School section. The claimant walks in a normal manner. The older male and female enter the church section.
(Portions on video)

10:08 AM: We enter the congregation and pew area of the church and find that the claimant and the children and the others are seated at a pew up front and cannot be seen without being next to them. We continue surveillance outside the church.

11:45 AM: The claimant and the children and the older couple exit the church. They walk to the KIA and enter it out of view due to the crowd dispersing. The older female drives them from the area.

11:56 AM: They arrive at 3085 Meridian Ave. They park and exit the SUV. The claimant and the children and the older couple walk a few yards and enter the restaurant.
(Portions on video)

12:06 PM: The claimant and her family are seated at a table and eating. There is no location for video availability. Surveillance is established outside the restaurant.

1:05 PM: The claimant and the others exit the restaurant and walk back to the KIA SUV. The claimant and the others enter the vehicle and the older female drives them from the area.
(Portions on video)

1:18 PM: They arrive at their residence and park in the driveway. The children and the older couple exit and enter the house. The claimant sits for a few moments and then gets out and enters the house and is out of view.
(Portions on video)

1:30 PM: Two of the children are playing outside on the lawn. The older male is with them.

2:11 PM: The children and the male are now inside the house.

3:00 PM: Surveillance is discontinued with the claimant at home.

NOTE: Approximately 2 minutes 49 seconds of video is obtained of the claimant walking and moving about without benefit of an orthopedic restraint on her right foot as prescribed.

CHAPTER NINE

TESTIFYING

There will come a time when in the course of a case, you will be required to testify in front of a judge and jury. You may also be deposed by opposing counsel. In all matters, you must be prepared and organized to relate the evidence of your investigation. You must be able to tell the details in a clear and concise manner.

Prior to the trial or deposition, carefully review your reports so that you are prepared to answer any and all questions. Make mental notes of all details. If you must write down your notes, be advised that opposing counsel has the right to look at your notes. And they WILL want to look at them.

Present yourself as the professional you are. Get a haircut. Wear a business suit/dress. Shine your shoes. Stand up straight. Get a good 's sleep and be rested. You represent yourself, your client, and all other Private Investigators.

Testifying at a Deposition

A Deposition is different from a jury trial. Depositions are especially useful to opposing counsel as they may ask questions that might not be allowed before a judge. Be assured that any answers you give during a deposition will be brought up at trial if there is any discrepancy. You will have to answer truthfully. In Worker's Compensation and Personal Injury Defense cases, you are not represented by Defense counsel. Defense counsel may object, but you will still have to answer the question. You basically are on your own. You may confer with Defense counsel, but they do NOT represent you. Be aware that Defense Investigator depositions typically last 4-6 hours and may go over to the next day. The process is grueling and takes a strong mind and determination to stand up for your client.

Always keep these points in mind when testifying at a Deposition:

- Be truthful. Be humble and dignified. Look the opposing counsel in the eye.
- Be aware that many Opposing Counsels employ "Videography" to videotape the witness for examination after the deposition to determine the witness' look if on the stand.
- Listen carefully and do not interrupt, even if you think you know the question.
- Pause. Defense Counsel may want a clarification.
- Pause Again. Think about your answer.
- Answer YES or NO. Do not explain. Do not guess. Do not exaggerate.
- Do not volunteer details.

- If you have to estimate, i.e., times or exact locations, be sure to state that your answer is an estimate.
- Avoid questions that are exact: "Do you always keep notes?".
- If you come to realize that you may have misspoke, correct yourself as soon as possible.
- Bring copies of requested documents only. No others should be offered.
- If you don't know details, do not offer to look for records
- Do not talk with opposing counsel afterwards. They are NOT your friend, they are their client's advocate and NOTHING is off the record.

Testifying at a Trial

- Keep in mind that in all Workers Compensation and Personal Injury claims, all evidence is Reciprocal Discovery and that any and all evidence that you have submitted, including Photographic, Video, and Written is already in possession of opposing counsel. There are no secrets allowed.
- All the Deposition advice stands true.

So, now you have to Testify in front of a Judge and Jury

- Sit in the witness seat like you've been there before. Sit up straight and look comfortable. Be confident. Be Positive. Speak Slowly, Clearly, and Loud enough for the jury to hear you.

- Client counsel will guide you through the time line/details of the investigation. Again, always listen to the question and answer, YES or NO, unless asked for details. Do Not exaggerate.
- Look at the jury when explaining explicit points.
- Opposing counsel will attempt to use prior deposition details and go even further to find a mistake in your testimony or confuse or upset you.
- Opposing counsel will question your experience. It's not personal.
- When questioned by opposing counsel, do not look at Defense Counsel or jury or judge. Look opposing counsel in the eye. Do not waffle, do not shrug shoulders, or roll your eyes.
- When playing back video evidence, do NOT narrate. If the Judge asks questions, answer to the best of your knowledge but do not offer an opinion.
- Be quick in getting your equipment on and off the viewing area.

Judgments in Workers Compensation and Personal Injury cases are decided by facts provided by Medical Professionals, Employers, Witnesses, and by Private Investigators.

Your work as an investigator is a part of a determination of fact and observation.

Your Testimony reflects the observation and circumstance of your investigation.

All you ever need to do is to tell the truth and offer evidence.

CHAPTER TEN

The Endgame: Ethics and Honor

Keep in mind that being a Private Investigator is an
evolving life. Laws change, technology upgrades every
few months, new equipment is available, and you must
progress with the times. The days of the lone wolf
private dick gumshoe in a trench coat are long gone and
have been replaced by professionals working with team
assets and an array of equipment. Continuing education
and involvement with trade associations such as
National Council of Investigation and Security Services
(NCISS) or state wide ones such as California Association
of Licensed Investigators (CALI) are essential to staying
current with the cause. There are periodicals like PI
Magazine and California Investigator that publish
monthly and quarterly that help in maintaining
knowledge.

One thing does NOT change!

Private Investigation is a profession that assists those
who may have no other advocate. KNOW your client.
Ask questions, be prepared to say, 'No". You may have
clients that are determined for an outcome, but You will
seek truth without favor. You should be aware of
circumstances that may be circumstantial. You will not
allow a client or a claimant or subject into a situation

that may cause harm to anyone. You will represent law and order and personal safety at all times.

The profession can be challenging and frustrating, but also rewarding and may allow you to have the satisfaction of helping others with knowing that you played a part in solving some of the mysteries of life.

Now, Go Forth and Multi-spy!

GLOSSARY SUB ROSA

A short list of useful Terms and Acronyms for the
beginning and professional
Private Investigator

AOE/COE *abbr*:   Arising from employment/condition
of employment. Worker's Compensation investigation
into the matter of the alleged injury at work

AME/QME *bar*: Agreed Medical Examiner/Qualified
Medical Examiner. Many times, a sub-rosa investigator
will be called upon to locate a claimant at a scheduled
medical appointment with an AME/QME. The
investigator should be prepared to wait. And wait. And
hope that the claimant goes straight home. Usually not.
Ever.

ANI *abbr*: Automated Number Identification index for
those who have DMV access. And you should.

Background *n*: Information concerning the case, usually
provided by the party paying. *See* True Background: The
information gathered by the investigator and that is
actually useful.

Bail:
  (1) The amount of money it takes to get a client out
      of jail (do not use your own bond)

  (2) Get out of the surveillance. It is not going well.

Break Off *v*: see Bail (2)

Bug Sweep *phrase*: See TSMC, or check your computer now...

Burn *v*:   The act of causing apprehension upon the part of the person being investigated or followed. Burnt *adj*: Too late, the person is on to you.

Claimant *n*: Worker's Compensation applicant

Client n: Beloved person(s) or entity that is willing to provide monetary compensation to investigators for devoted determination and results. These people are rare and should be considered with delicate and profound appreciation.

Contact *n* or *v*:   Contact is mostly used as a term to make a personal investigation by various means for various reasons. It usually indicates that the investigator has used a ruse to determine the Claimant/Subject identity or whereabouts. It is used for talking to neighbors and associates when talking with them personally. *See*: Pretext: Door knock, Telephone

Database n: A collection of information stored on computers. Helpful when trying to gather but be when advising clients. Always verify!

Domestic *n*: Describes a case that involves dispute between couples, may include marriage/divorce/child protection. Should include special consideration and a payment up front to investigator.

Door Knock n: A Pretext (*see* Pretext) investigation where in the investigator knocks on a door of a residence to locate the claimant/subject. The key is to have knowledge of the kind of catch needed.

E&O *abbr*: Errors and Omission Insurance. You will need insurance. Trust me.

EDEX *abbr*: Electronic Data Exchange System for CA Worker's Compensation cases. Must be an approved subscriber!

EE *abbr*: Employee

FRCA abbr: Fair Credit and Reporting Act. If you use any commercial database search, or if on your own—you need to know this law concerning what is available to you, your clients, and what you can report.

Hinky *adj*: Claimant may be aware of surveillance or may be merely odd. This comes up a lot.

Locate *v* or *n*: To find an object, an address, or a Claimant/Subject. Usually because the Claimant/Subject prefers not to be found.

Health Hints for the Sub-rosa Operative

Thinking of specializing in surveillance? Sub-rosa/Surveillance investigations bring several commands to the field operative. Long hours, physical skills and uncomfortable positions are part and parcel of any assignment. These tips are for those who accept the challenge of chasing your prey and meeting your client's requirements.

First and foremost, <u>START HEALTHY!</u> Before you begin a career as an investigator, have a physical and know your body, yourself. You must be able to sit for long periods, able to move quickly, ~~to~~ walk, hike, run, stop and recover all within a few moments. You may have to climb a tree, run up Russian Hill, rollerblade the promenade, spin around and duck down, stop and start to do your thing until your heart is like a hummingbird wing. Your mind must be attentive, your eyes clear, your ears open. You may have to carry equipment and use it on the fly. Sleep and rest is primary before starting a new assignment. You will most likely have to begin your day very early and stay very late. It will be understood that you can perform at all hours and at all times.

Let's start with the Sub-rosa Operative Essential Tools.

Vehicle Essentials:

- PortaPotty for waste deposal. There are several units of varying sizes that will fit your vehicle. At the least, carry a container for fluids.
- First Aid Kit
- Portable fan, handheld
- Cold bag w/ice
- Sunscreen as even darkened windows will not completely protect you
- Neck rest
- Lumbar support
- Loose clothing as sitting for long periods may restrict blood stream
- Water and snacks. (Salty snacks will do you no good!) Bits of fruit, trail mix, energy bars that have nuts or other types of protein, are best.
- Remember, it will be hotter by at least 10-15 degrees inside your vehicle than it is outside. Heat will make your blood pressure/pulse rate rise and cause dehydration.
- Running your vehicle's air conditioner while on stationary surveillance is usually not practical. It may alert others to your presence and/or damage your vehicle.

Some ways to keep cool:

- Swamp cooler - There are models that may fit your vehicle
- Neck cooler - There are cloth wraps that can be wetted and frozen and used around your neck.

- Personal battery operated fan
- Ice packs
- Ice chips kept in a cold bag and used to kept your mouth from drying out

NOTE: If you feel overly heated and are lightheaded, you may have to move from your stationary position and seek relief from the heat. Your health and well-being is most important. (Although I know most of us sacrifice ourselves in the "heat" of the moment just to get that perfect shot.)

Personal Essentials:

- A supply of Medications in case you are unexpectedly sent out of town
- Second pair of glasses or contacts/ eyewash etc.
- Tissues/wet naps/paper towels
- Change of clothing
- Small but nutritious bits of food for breakfast, lunch, or dinner. It is not recommended that you eat large amounts during Sub-rosa Investigations for obvious reasons.

Sub-rosa Surveillance can be stressful. You will be hyper-aware for hours at a time and it will wear on you. It helps to have a Zen-like calm personality, but those of us who do not, here are some suggestions:

- Meditation practice assists in concentrating at the matter at hand. Some find that Meditation and/or Yoga classes and exercise works for surveillance and keeping limber
- If possible, get out and walk around your vehicle every hour or so. This alleviates muscle cramps and provides blood flow
- Try Isometric exercises while seated. It helps with concentration and calorie burn

These are examples and experiences of a career in Sub-rosa Surveillance and are not meant to be offered as medical advice. You will find what best works for you in your journey as an investigator. Safety and health are sometimes set aside in our profession. Let us not forget that we are needed for the next case, too.

ABOUT THE AUTHOR

Robert Estes is a native born Northern Californian with 35 years of experience as a Private Investigator specializing in Workers' Compensation Fraud, Personal Injury, and Criminal and Civil Litigation. He has written many articles for publication and has lectured on the topics. Robert still gets up in the morning excited about what the day will bring because as an investigator, every day is different and has its own challenges and rewards.

Robert Estes Investigations located in California with offices in Santa Rosa, San Jose, and Pasadena. He may be contacted through his website at www.norcalpi.net

www.ingramcontent.com/pod-product-compliance
Lightning Source LLC
Chambersburg PA
CBHW061222180526
45170CB00003B/1110